THE TEN COMMANDMENTS OF EXCELLENCE

EXCERPT: COMMANDMENTS 2 & 5

C.L. LAWRENCE

Fallon House Publishers, LLC
New Jersey

International Standard Book Number
ISBN- 978-0-9972082-8-3
Printed in the United States of America

First Printing 2016

Fallon House Publishing
P.O. Box 220
Oaklyn, NJ 08107

LawrenceMinistries.com

Ordering Information
Amazon Author Central: amazon.com/author/cllawrence
Quantity sales. Special discounts are available on quantity purchases by corporations, associations, and others. For details, contact: cll@LawrenceMinistries.com

DEDICATED TO

The Rev. Dr. Donald Sullivan Medley

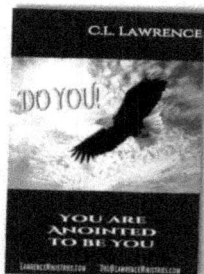

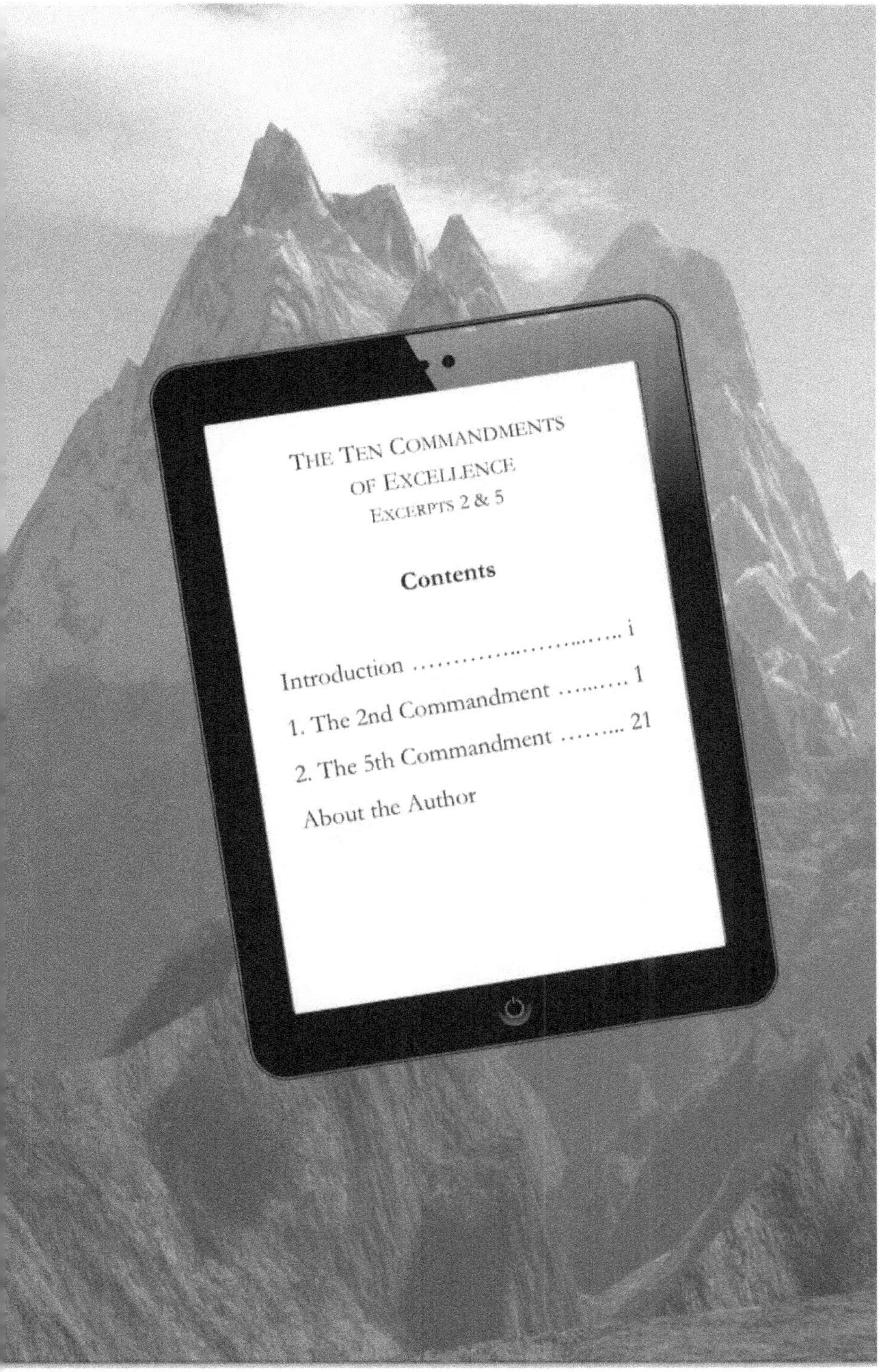
THE TEN COMMANDMENTS
OF EXCELLENCE
EXCERPTS 2 & 5
Contents
Introduction …………..……..….. i
1. The 2nd Commandment …..…. 1
2. The 5th Commandment ……... 21
About the Author

ACKNOWLEDGMENTS

Two women of God whose presence of poise, grace and elegance in the pulpit is eclipsed only by their powerfully anointed preaching.

Rev. Dr. Prathia L. Hall (January 1, 1940 – August 12, 2002), leader and activist in the Civil Rights Movement, womanist theologian, and ethicist. The Elijah in my life, who taught me to go beyond "flat reading," walk circumspectly between the lines of the text to see the unseen; and to ask God for the voice of the people. She opened my eyes to a boundless world view that finds relevance and reason in the Word in any context. I honor and cherish the memory of her mother love, as sister/friend and unselfish mentorship that influenced my life and ministry beyond measure.

Bishop, Dr. Millicent H. Hunter, Sr. Pastor of the Baptist Worship Center Church, Philadelphia, PA and Presiding Prelate of the Worship Center World Wide Fellowship of Churches. Her example of relentless commitment and unquestioning obedience to God has shown me the endless possibilities of God's purpose for those who dare to believe for more. When they said, she shouldn't, she pursued. When they said, she couldn't, she did. Beneath the weight of every test and trial, disappointment, and setback, through struggles and pain, she embodied Maya Angelou's "Still I Rise."

INTRODUCTION

There are six entities involved in the domain of preaching, (1) God, the Father, (2) God, the Son, Jesus, (3) God, the Holy Spirit, (4) the written Word of God, (5) the hearer, and (6) the preacher, the vessel. No one would argue the supremacy and divine authority of the first four, the Divine Entities; or the importance of the fifth, the people. While this book acknowledges each, the passionate concern of this writing is for the person of the preacher. The preacher is expected to be a finely tuned vessel through whom living waters flow; able to meet the intellectual expectations of homiletics, hermeneutics, astutely interpret the integration of culture and Word, while staying humble in the unspoken impact of pulpit presence. All of that is a part of preaching so this book has everything to do with preaching.

I pastored a church in the early 2000s. After about three months I found out the true story of the well-guarded secret of my predecessor's departure. Suicide. There's much that could be read into the details but the point is, he took his life. A man of God, pastor of a respected church, took his life. That experience heightened my passionate concern for the dynamics within and around "the person of the preacher." The preacher as a person gets little attention until scandal erupts, or the high rate of suicide among preachers is noticed, or an article is written about the mass exit of clergy back into the secular workforce.

All after the fact. What about nuances that matter but overlooked because, shall we say, the tyranny of the urgent.

OK! There you are! Called to preach, uniquely gifted, anointed, armed and fully clad in the whole armor of God. Seminary behind you, visions before you, Bible apps on all your smart devices. Have Sermon Will Travel! Ready to preach in season and out of season. But wait! There are a few things you need to know before you go; things they don't tell you in seminary or Bible institutes. As a preacher, you may be in positions other than pastor, but you're still perceived as a leader. Though differing across denominations and culture, there're certain perceptions and responsibilities that come with the call. You'll learn as you go but OJT (On the Job Training), as in the secular arena, has limitations. Mistakes are costly, and sad as it is, sometimes unforgiven. You would be wise to learn from the experience of seasoned others who desire your highest good.

The Ten Commandments of Excellence is a canon of fundamental ethical principles invaluable to preachers at every level of experience. Excellence doesn't happen by prayer alone but by the deliberate embrace and continued practice of precepts that prepare and position you to be exalted by the Holy Spirit in your due season. The powerful principles shared in the following pages aren't secrets, but overlooked and often underestimated tenets that can shape, perfect and sustain you throughout your ministerial journey.

In the Hollywood movie, The Ten Commandments,[a] Moses, portrayed by Charlton Heston, came down from Mt. Sinai, hair white, face aglow, the Ten Commandments etched on two tablets of stone braced in his arms, saying he'd been in the presence of God. Today The Ten Commandments of Excellence can be downloaded to your handheld devices, or bound between the cover of a book. Your hair, probably, won't

---

[a] The Ten Commandments 1956 epic film produced and directed by Cecil B. DeMille

turn white and without the aid of cosmetics you'll probably not have that "Moses glow" depicted in the movie. But, if in the pursuit of excellence, you internalize The Ten Commandments of Excellence, you'll glow with God's favor as you excel beyond the level of mediocrity in your call to preach the Good News in the Word of God.

I wrote The Ten Commandments of Excellence because you asked me to. After every leadership seminar, conference, and training session, I'd prayerfully ponder the thoughts and questions shared, hoping I'd added meaningful value beyond that of a great learning experience. Finally, there was an undeniable God breathed voice in my spirit, "You have your assignment; just do it."

Rabbi Zusya (1718–1800), an Orthodox rabbi and an early Hasidic luminary was renowned throughout the world for his insights as a scholar, teacher, and healer. When he was an old man he grew nervous as he thought about the world to come, his life and how little he had done. He began to imagine what the angel who would meet him might ask.

"Why were you not a Moses?" He thought, I shall answer with conviction, 'Because I was not born to be a Moses.' "And if the angel challenges me, 'But neither did you perform the feats of Elijah.' Again, he thought, I shall firmly respond, 'My mission was not the same as that of Elijah." But there is one question he feared God would ask and he'd be unable to answer: Why were you not a Rabbi Zusya?

THE 2ND COMMANDMENT
THOU SHALL BE THINE
AUTHENTIC SELF

T HINK FOR A MOMENT. ARE YOU BEING your real self? Do you know? The question has nothing to do with wigs, toupees, cosmetic enhancements, or anything related to outward appearance. Those things are your choices, adornments that change with styles and fashion. Your authentic self is what lives vibrantly through or lies silently beneath what's visible. Authenticity means genuine; real; not false or copied. What was first, at the root, the core? What was there before anything else ever was? Authenticity, then, begins with who God created you to be; who you are on the inside. Your authentic self is the genuine you, not a copy of someone else, who you look like or what you do for a living. Your authentic self is your unique you, who you are, your passions, values, what you think, how you think, how you process and interact with the world, your personality, temperament, and disposition. Your authenticity begins with God.

Are you a patient person? A tolerant person? A compassionate person? Are you free spirited, comfortable with ambiguity, or do you prefer structure? Are you an "inside the box" or an "outside the box" person? Are you laid back or assertive? Are you a nine to five person or do you work until the

1

job is done? Do you naturally take the lead in situations even without the title? The questions can go on and on. There is no subliminal judgment in any of the questions, no good or bad, right, or wrong. Everyone is different; everyone is valid in their personality, style; their created being. Every person is a creative expression of God's image, each reflecting parts of the infinite facets of God's self.

There are several instruments that define personality types, work styles, leadership styles, etc. While you don't want to get bogged down or obsessed with the instruments, they're helpful in a couple of ways. While not culturally objective, they present an outline of the personality and leadership styles, giving you a larger view of the array of types and where you may theoretically find your definition. Consistent with your level of open-mindedness, engaging in the instruments can be intimidating or informative. Have fun with them. They're not meant to be conclusive, only thought provoking. Approach them broadmindedly, without preconceived notions and that will decrease the element of judgment and bias normally brought to an experience. View the results as a guide or a window through which to gain insight into yourself. No one, except God, knows you better than you do. Personality and work style instrument often help you to get to know yourself a little better.

Secondly, it's important to have a general understanding of your personality type. It goes a long way in learning to accept and appreciate yourself, the person God created. It also helps in the understanding of the unique ways in which the Holy Spirit guides and uses you in the Kingdom of God.

Being your authentic self is living from the inside out, interacting with the world through the lens and grid of who you really are. Who you are on the inside has nothing to do with what others are thinking or saying about you. Your authentic self is the "you" who never changes. You may hide your you, disguise your you, or even try to kill your you by trying to be someone else, but your authentic self will always be there waiting for affirmation and opportunities for expression. There is a need for the real you in the world or God would not have bothered to create you if you weren't somehow necessary in his overall eternal plan. You have a voice that only certain one's can hear. You have a style that only certain ones can relate to. You have "a way" that only certain ones will follow. Paul says, God will supply all of our needs. You are the need of someone or something in God's plan. Start wrapping your mind around that thought. No, you're not the "itness of the allness," or the "end all to be all," but recognizing the intentionality of your being is the perfect place to begin. God, our creator, uniquely designed every person. He wasn't having a bad day when he came up with your blueprint. You're not a mistake, an "OOPS!" or afterthought, substitute, or an addendum, but part of the divine tapestry of time, the bigger picture, set in motion before the foundation of the world. You have a specific purpose, a strategic part, a role to play in the drama of eternity, but to see the beauty of it all you must come unpretentiously to the life experience. It's a choice.

To come to the life experience unpretentiously is a choice

Consider for a moment, Spiritual Gifts. Paul takes time to talk about spiritual gifts and the precision of their operation. Insight reveals that while different personality types operate in each of the gifts, there are certain personality types more suited for certain gifts. Being your authentic self, the self who God created in you positions you to function with excellence in your respective spiritual gift(s) and calling.

There is a cultural habit of comparing one's self to others; against biased standards of beauty; socially defined definitions of success and accomplishment; against others who've reached a level of celebrity or notoriety to which one may admire or aspire. At an early age, well-meaning voices dictate

3

what to think of yourself, what the world thinks of you, what to think of the world around you and how to fit into it, … or not. Nurturing, social grooming, mentoring is good and necessary, and you're blessed when it comes from those who love and desire to see you grow into your best self. Be aware, however, there are other voices eager to be heard, shaping your perceptions with the fruit of their life experience of narrow vision, dwarfed goals, and sight walking. Rhetoric that constructs walls around you, giving you a box to live in, fostering a world view limited to their own.

Sound bites, highway billboards, overt and covert messages coming at you every minute of the day telling you how you ought to look, how you should think and feel, what you should buy, and what/who you ought to be. Carefully crafted marketing strategies using subliminal suggestions that feed your demons of destructive self-images, self-hatred, self-doubt and low self-esteem plant the seeds of inadequacy watered with doubt, artfully conspiring to convince you, first, that there is a problem, and, secondly, that the problem is "You." You're not good enough. You need to be a better you, a more appealing you, a more successful you. You're too much of this or not enough of that, but there's a solution just for you that will bring you to that subjective standard of "perfection." The message is clear: You aren't good enough as you are. You need to be fixed. Truth is not the measure and reality is not the issue. Keeping you focused outwardly is the means to prevent you from seeing inwardly, blinding you to your inner treasure and the beauty of your authentic self.

Many spend their lifetime trying to find someone else to be, copying this one and mimicking that one, thinking someone

> Many spend a lifetime trying to find someone else to be

else is somehow better. So deeply rooted that it becomes second nature to look outwardly for the solution to becoming "the better you." So much a part of your sub consciousness that you pass it down to your children. So engrained in your psyche that you judge yourself and others by the perceptions continuously cultivated in your minds over your lifetime.

It's no wonder precious people of God lose their sense of themselves long before ever having an opportunity to become aware of their true selves and appreciate who they are as a wonderful, planned creation of God with a divine purpose and an intentional future. You are anointed to be you. You're your own worst critic, finding what you perceive as flaws in yourself, even sometimes asking God why he made you this way. BUT! to whom are you comparing yourself? Against whose standard are you measuring yourself? Certainly, you should smooth edges and rid yourself of destructive behaviors and habits that masquerade as second nature. You should stir up and perfect your gifts and talents, but surely not change who you are. You're not approved because you're perfect, you're approved because of to whom you belong. To be your authentic self you have to know your you, and accept yourself as a good product of God's work that day; the reality of his imagination, perfect imperfections, flaws and all. Whatever you are, too much of this and not enough of that, you are perfectly shaped and fashioned to do what you were created to do.

You are anointed to be you

The desire to matter, fit in, be accepted, have recognition, a sense of purpose and belonging can be very strong, leading you to become unduly influenced, giving up your capacity of pure, free, independent thought to the degree necessary to feel accepted and affirmed. Using a grassroots term, that's "selling yourself cheap." When

Identity Theft

you relinquish your power of self-validation to others, adapting yourself to what you think you should be without giving yourself the benefit of seeking to know and cultivate the person God has created you to be; without a positive, healthy and confident self-awareness, you will seek to be someone else; a copycat; a fraud. No! No! No! That's **Identity Theft.** A borrowed identity just won't do. To find value in being someone else is an insult to your authentic self, as well as the God who made you.

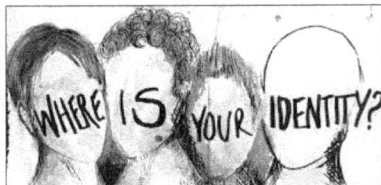

You may be inspired by others and try to develop similar qualities of character, but those qualities will be expressed through your own person. When you're content with yourself, comfortable in your own skin, you don't compare or compete with others. You can look with admiration at others, their accomplishments, and elevations, hear the accolades and applause, and be genuinely happy for them without feeling slighted or passed over. It's in the knowing that "what God has for you is for you. It's in knowing your spiritual gifts and calling, passion and purpose that allows you to rise above the low state of envy and jealousy because you know who you are in Christ. When you're not trying to be something or someone you're not, there's an incredible peace that abides on the inside, and rest from having to be "on" all the time.

What is Your Authentic Self?

"I am nobody but myself."
-- Ralph Ellison

When you set yourself free to be yourself, you never have to think about how to be yourself. You just do what comes naturally. Do you! "Free to be me" isn't that self-indulgent philosophy of hedonism. It's a mental posture that allows the freedom to grow into what God would have you to be, and finding joy in being that.

Children get it, but somewhere along the way, lose it. Listen to this funny but insightful wisdom in an exchange between three children as one was teasing and mimicking the other:

Lex: **Don't copy me!**

Nip: But you're so cute.

Lex: **I know, but you don't get to be cute by being a copycat.**

Nip: OK, then how did you get so cute?

Lex: **God made me that way. That's how.**

Nip: How can I get cute like you?

Lex: **You can't get cute like me, Boo. You have to get cute like you. That's the way God works.**

Dove: That's right, and God made me cuter than all y'all!

Your authentic self is your "cute." It's your "you;" your unique you. You know when you've found your cute when you can say, I'm okay with me. I'm comfortable with me. I like me.

Authenticity is an easy concept to entertain when talking about artwork or antiques; but not so easy in the context of self and on the very personal level of self-examination. What does the real you look like? What makes you uniquely you? Even the thought of engaging in self-exploration to answer those questions can be quite intimidating. You don't know what or who you might find. Suppose "I don't like what I find?" Ok, that's an understandable fear. Remember, everything starts with God. In Genesis chapter one, in the beginning of all creation, as God completed the various entities it tells us that he saw that "it was good." Say it with me, "I'm the manifestation of God's creative imagination." When he finished creating you, he saw that you were good. He likes what he did. He loves you. The Holy Spirit will guide you to a new and true vision of yourself as you make finding, accepting and being your authentic self an intentional part of your spiritual development.

What does authenticity have to do with preaching?

It has much to do with preaching. The preacher is the bearer of the message. The sermon begins before the preacher opens his or her mouth. You speak before you say a word. Authenticity speaks with a loud voice. It attracts others. People are drawn to those who are comfortable in their own skin. Others feel comfortable and secure in your self-confidence. If you're masquerading as someone else, perhaps a preacher you admire or one whose success you desire, then you're always acting, never being.

How can you preach about a creative God if you can't live in the uniqueness he created in you?

The absence of authenticity brings the sermon into question. Is the sermon you're preaching one that drawn breath in your spirit first? Are you re-preaching a sermon that "worked" for another preacher. If the sermon begins before you say a word, then everything about you is an introduction to the sermon and part of the sermon. Your style. Is it you? Or are you copying someone else? Your speech. Is it you? Or are you mimicking someone else? Your delivery. Is it you? Or are you channeling someone else? How can you preach about a creative God without living out the uniqueness within yourself.? God never meant for you to be the same as any other preacher or he could have created clones. God created all things, distinction in all things and beauty in the distinction. What is your distinction? What makes you distinctively, authentically you?

Your personality, your approach to life in general, what you bring to the scripture largely determines what you look for in the scriptures and what you bring out of it. Some things you just can't fake no matter how hard you try. You may imitate preaching style, physical expressions, voice inflections, even little idioms from another preacher but imitation becomes transparent when it comes to the message. You can't preach with authenticity what you don't believe, what you don't embrace within yourself. You may give sound to the words but you can't fake authenticity and without authenticity there is no power. You may turn up the volume but there will be no power. In other words, a negative, grumpy person can't preach about joy with any degree of spiritual integrity. No one would believe them. A judgmental person will have difficulty preaching about the blessedness of God's outpouring of grace and favor, and the free gift of salvation because a judgmental preacher wants you to pay for your sins and wear your sorrow.

If you're an old fogy, fuddy duddy, who holds onto the way things used to be (and you can be that at 35 years old), you can't preach about the new things waiting in an exciting new future. You can't preach Isaiah 42:9 or 43:19. How can you embrace the tools of technology, and social media if you're holding fast to the past? You can't preach what you can't embrace. You can't preach what you don't have in you because the thinly veiled façade soon breaks down. Authenticity has everything to do with preaching.

Finding Your Own Voice

Your voice begins with God. Voice in this context isn't the audible sound that comes out of your mouth when you preach; it isn't volume or decibels. Your voice is your interpretations; the result of that which flows through your unique grid system on its way to becoming speech. Your voice begins with you in the Potter's hand; God molding and distinctively creating not just the vessel but the way the vessel receives, digests thoughts and feels. You're recognizable by what you say and how you say it. Your voice is distinctive. It's your signature. It's the sound of your personality, your personalized way of interpreting things and presenting them. Your voice reflects your passions, gifts, that about which you care deeply, the totality of your life experiences; your testimonies, and the wisdom you've gained from your joys and sorrows; so much so that the Holy Spirit can use any or all of it to empower the Word you preach. Your voice is what makes your message particular and alive. Someone can take five of your sermons, and given you haven't stolen them from another preacher,[b] they can get a sense of who you are.

Read this paragraph carefully with an open mind. The Bible says in both accounts of the Gospel, Matthew and Luke that what comes out of our mouths is that which is in our heart. This is, in part, why different preachers can preach from the identical text and the sermon come across differently. Without knowing it, the preacher relates to or finds something of himself or herself in the text. Subconsciously or not, regardless of the amount of study the preacher runs the text through their personal grid system and what comes out has a little or a lot of themselves woven into the sermon. Back in the old days there were preachers known as "sin preachers." They could find sin in the way you brushed your teeth, highly judgmental, very limited on grace. They could make forgiveness so conditional that it sounded more like a threat. You knew them. You didn't have to go to the revival to know what they were going to preach. You knew their voice. There were no "grace notes" in the melody of their messages. Conversely, another preacher could

---

[b] The 8th Commandment, Thou Shall Not Steal

preach about sin and make you happy to repent because of the way they presented grace. That's voice.

The buzz word is "brand." Your voice is your brand. Is your voice familiar even to you? How would you describe your brand? If your life could speak, what would it say? What are you known for as a preacher in the kingdom realm? If you were an instrument, which one would it be and how would you sound? Poignant questions yet many preachers exhaust themselves hiding in someone else's brand, never asking the questions. Be bold. Ask the questions, then take the time to answer yourself.

What do I think about this or that? My opinions, the things I espouse and express; are they what I believe or what's been passed down to me or I've heard from others? Is it what my mind, my spirit, and my emotions have discussed with the scriptures? Do I know my own mind? Does this really sound like me? That will be revisited a little later in this section.

Finding your voice means discovering your comfort zone, the courage to give full expression in your sermons through your true self. It's about the story you tell (message) and how you tell it (voice). When you think of your voice, think of your purpose. Is it to motivate, inspire, teach, challenge, comfort encourage, empower, ...? Your purpose will come through in your messages. The Biblical stories have been told thousands of times, through thousands of messages and messengers over thousands of years. In preaching, your message isn't just words on a manuscript, it's God's message communicated through your voice. No one can say it the way you say it. No one can feel the meaning and express it the way you can.

Developing your authentic voice takes time, courage, and practice. It means overcoming the fear of being yourself and letting go of what others think is "preaching." Sometimes you don't yet know what your true voice sounds like because you've been mimicking others for so long; preaching it like Bishop Rev. Dr. Wonderful. It takes self-excavation, daring to discover what you have buried deep within, or what has been buried by any number of influences around you: culture, church, workplace, family. When you can understand that you have a voice that is exclusively yours to develop and to share, you'll stop allowing yourself to be diminished by mimicking the voice of others. You'll no longer define yourself in comparison to another preacher or based on what others are doing or saying. The next time you feel yourself starting to compare yourself to others, **STOP!** Remind yourself that you have your own voice, unique to you, to your message, and to your calling.

On the day of Pentecost, the Holy Spirit made quite a dramatic entrance into the upper room. The sound of a mighty rushing wind, tongues of fire. WOW! A diverse multitude of people heard the Gospel in the language of their own nationality or ethnicity. There was only one preacher and the Holy Spirit allowed the Gospel to be heard in many languages. Amazing.

Let's step out of the box and stretch our thoughts a little bit to see how that may apply within the framework of our concern. While there's one Holy Spirit, there's diversity within the body of Christ, the ear of the soul and the language the soul understands. It isn't a language you can study or learn. It's language that emanates from your being. Just as teaching styles have been adapted to address different learning styles, so God created you, unique in your language to resonate with the diversity of his hearers. Authenticity is your divine responsibility to God, yourself, and for the sake of others whom you're meticulously designed to serve.

There are those who will only hear the message of the Gospel in the language of your speech, your voice. Not talking about the language of a nationality (African, French, German, …) but your language, that which is filtered through the wisdom gleaned from the testimony of your life journey. Your voice doesn't change the story; it doesn't change the truth but it changes how the story is told. It may include passion and compassion not experienced by others, yet which makes the story audible to someone who otherwise couldn't hear it. If you're a copycat, then all those whom you were created to bless will be robbed of what was meant for them. God supplies every need. Your voice is the supply of someone's need.

There's no one else like you. There's a musical sound in you that is your own. A rhythm that emanates from your soul. A melody in the lyrics of your speech. The rhythm, the melody, and the lyrics create a symphonic language that is uniquely yours. It takes an emotionally secure, spiritually mature person to hear and appreciate their symphony and say within, I like the song born in my soul. When you hear it, that's when you've heard your own voice.

Your voice is the supply of someone's need

Let's revisit the question, "Do I know my own mind?" from the perspective of what it has to do with preaching. A question not to be answered hastily. The question isn't to suggest that you preach your own opinion, but to examine how you process the truths that lie before you and how you interpret matters in a time of change, in a world of broad exposure and intellectual access.

Volumes can be written on how times have changed; how the world has changed. Norms, values, beliefs, rules, ideologies, philosophies, continue to be challenged more quickly and dramatically than ever in the history of humanity. There is the thought, however, that things and people have not changed all that much. Cyberspace has created a global community exposing you to information previously unavailable. As a global citizen, you're exposed to information that sharpens your insight, expands your world view, and your thinking. That which existed without your knowledge is now in your personal space. You can no longer rest in the comfort of limited thoughts, experiences, and opinions, regurgitating what you've heard.

The information super highway has changed and challenged our reality on every level. Every belief is confronted and tested. The world will never be the same, and that's exciting. With all the change, however, the preacher is called to proclaim an unchanged Gospel in a language that speaks its relevance to a world that is different in ways unfamiliar to our experience. The prevailing thought or interpretations through the grid from years gone by may be too narrow for the larger landscape in which you now live. They may or may not be relevant or absolute in this regard: It may be conclusive based on the information available in a time and a particular social location. Yes, truth is what it is and does not change, but, revelation is God's prerogative. Be cautious of the arrogance to believe that in the breadth of your finite thinking; in the nanosecond of time you occupy in eternity, that you hold the complete volume of eternal truth. As time peels back layers of reality, a larger view brings greater light. That which was previously thought to be conclusive gives way to new considerations, new thoughts revelatory of a bigger and greater God.

You are called to a specific moment in history. You weren't born or called in the horse and buggy day, or the days of only snail mail and 10 cents per call phone booths on the street. You're called in the age of technology. Silicon Valley has given the world tools never imagined even 20 years ago. The Internet has made it possible to experience new horizons, exposed diversity and challenges to faith and Christian values. That alone is God pealing back more layers of himself for you to experience. You can no longer relax in the comfort zone of neighborhood thinking; rest in the familiarity of limited thoughts, experiences, and opinions. The world is at your doorstep, in your living room, on the smart devices your children hold in their hands and the social networks with which no one can keep up. You're called to reach a generation that no longer lives in the neighborhood but the world. Called in this generation to the awareness of the globalism and all the implications and applications. The information super highway has changed and challenged our reality on every level. Every belief is challenged and tested. The world will never be the same. Things once hidden are now vying to be normative. What someone else thought about something may not be what resonates in that place where God speaks in your spirit.

You are trusted with the truth in the time in which you live. Congregations that sit before you aren't the congregations of "Ozzie & Harriet" or "Father Knows Best." of yester year. Education, information and social location, change thinking. No, you're not called to change the truth but to give it a voice that's comprehensible. Examine and re-examine the challenges before you. It's not the message that needs to be changed because truth endures through all generations, but the voice God requires in such a time as this may be different. If may be yours. In the pursuit of your own voice, do you have the courage to accept the challenges to the things you've believed in and see what's left standing? There may be a difference in what you've been preaching when you were not in your authentic self. Have you the courage to give your own thoughts a second thought? Think about it.

Who do people say that I am?

Jesus and his disciples left Galilee and went up to the villages near Caesarea Philippi. As they were walking along, he asked them, "Who do people say I am?" Mark 8:27 NLT

Departing from the traditional interpretation of this scripture and using Jesus' question to illustrate a thought that can be extracted as a sub context, Jesus wasn't asking about the "buzz." He knew the people were talking about him, what they'd witnessed, what they'd heard and what they'd experienced. You can imagine with all he'd done; he would wonder how that translated in the people's minds. Were they "getting it?" He wasn't asking about what they thought of his deeds. He asked is disciples specifically not "what," but "who" the people were saying he was. Then he asked an even more poignant question, "Who do YOU say that I am?"

When Jesus was with the multitudes in the villages and on the outskirts of the cities he was healing and teaching. That was the perception of him some of the people had; healer, teacher. He was with his disciples day and night. They knew him up close and personal. He was asking if there was harmony between the man the people saw and the man the disciples knew; between his public persona and the man he was in his personal circle. Perhaps he was more concerned about who the disciples thought he was. Nevertheless, his question poses a sub context: Is everyone seeing the same thing? It takes a bit of courage to go there. Can people trust who/what they see? Authenticity is a matter of integrity. Dare to think about it and ask yourself some questions. Who am I? Am I projecting my authentic self or a copy of someone else? Am I coming across the way I hope that I am?

To be your authentic self you must be well acquainted with your-self, and accept yourself as a product of God's handiwork; perfections and perfect imperfections. An insecure person with difficulty accepting him/herself, with a flawed sense of self-worth and unhealed wounds cannot be a servant else they will use and abuse the people of God to meet their own needs. A person dissatisfied with their self will try to find someone else to be.

> Who do people say
> you are?
>
> Can they trust
> what they see?

Consider spiritual gifts within the framework of this discussion. Think of them in terms of being a part of a larger whole, the big picture of God's human tapestry. Positioning yourself in that framework will open your eyes as to how and where you fit in. Think of yourself in practical terms; your personality, habits, tendencies, attitudes, etc. What excites you and motivates you? What makes your heart sing?

You are who you are. God created you so you're in his plan. He can use you if you are willing to be your authentic self.

NOTES

PRAYERFULLY PONDER

1. What's unique about you?

_____

_____

_____

_____

_____

2. What are you known for?

_____

_____

_____

_____

_____

3. What are your spiritual gifts? How do you use them?

_____

_____

_____

_____

_____

NOTES

"If you know the enemy and know yourself, you need not fear the result of a hundred battles. If you know yourself but not the enemy, for every victory gained you will also suffer a defeat. If you know neither the enemy nor yourself, you will succumb in every battle."

— Sun Tzu, The Art of War

THE 5ᵀᴴ COMMANDMENT

THOU SHALL FLEE JEALOUSY & ENVY

M EET THE INFAMOUS SERIAL KILLERS, jealousy and envy. They travel together, look alike, often behave alike, people confuse them, but make no mistake. They're different. It's well worth your time to know them and clearly recognize the distinct difference between the two because left unleashed these two emotions are very formidable enemies, skillfully stealth in taking down kings and queens, destroying nations and killing hopes and dreams without shedding one drop of blood, although they have been known to be the impetus behind malicious criminal behavior, even murder. Because this book is for preachers, the two concepts are confined within the context of church life, but think not for a moment they behave differently in the Kingdom of God than in the natural world. They'll sucker punch anyone regardless of where they are or who they are.

In the fifth chapter of the first letter that bears his name, Peter issues a wake-up call using two strong words, sober and vigilant. To be sober is to be clear minded and free from the influence of anything mind altering. Vigilant is to be watchful and cautious. You need to be sober and vigilant at all times in this call. Use your sanctified imagination and envision twin lions,

Envy and Jealousy, stalking you day and night. The surest path to defeat in any adversarial situation is to underestimate your enemy. Don't make that mistake with these two. Envy and jealousy are emotions, deceptively similar but different. In one way, they are even each other's opposite: envy is evoked when someone has something good that you want, jealousy when you have something good that you believe someone else wants to have. Envy involves a longing for what you don't have.

- If you crave a mega church like Bishop Awesome, you're envious of Bishop Awesome.

- If you're upset about losing your members to Bishop Awesome, you're jealous.

Emotions are powerful. With equal dexterity, they can motivate you to greatness with enthusiasm or to destruction with the ease and precision of a lion's powerful swipe.

Both these emotions lie within the flesh to a greater or lesser degree. The frequency and intensity of their appearance is primarily contingent upon individual personality, temperament, the way one looks at the world, and spiritual maturity. While the call to preach is a divine call, it falls upon the human vessel, therefore subjecting it to the preacher's internal struggles, the war between the flesh and the spirit which Paul so thoroughly and eloquently describes in Romans 12:14-24. It's important to understand from two vantage points and multiple perspectives how envy and jealousy operate. You can be jealous or envious, or the object of someone's jealousy or envy. Both emotions are considered here.

ENVY

To feel envious of someone, you need to compare yourself to that person. You can envy someone's intelligence, good looks, social position, or relationship with a person. In each of these cases, you determine that the other person is better off than you, and that you would want that good thing for yourself. Psychologists suggest there are two types of envy: Benign Envy and Malicious Envy.

When You Envy Others (Benign Envy: The Safe Zone)

Benign envy is the kind which raises you up rather than making you want to pull the other person down. It carries a positive connotation, a type of emotional stimulus that moves the person to aspire to be as good in whatever way as the object of their envy. It can be used to express a desire to equal another in achievement or excellence as in emulation or admiration. In this notion, it's used in a complimentary sense without negative implications. If you say, "I envy the way Rev. Grey can paint a vivid picture as he preaches," this is a positive statement, quite complimentary. If you stop there, you're in the safe zone. There is, however, a very fine line separating the Safe Zone from the Danger Zone.

When You Envy Others (Malicious Envy: The Danger Zone)

We tend to feel malicious envy towards another person if we think their success is undeserved. This is the type that makes us want to strike out at the other person and bring them down a peg or two. Malicious envy also includes the judgment that the other person does not deserve the good thing, so not only do you want to have the object for yourself, you also want the other person to not have it anymore.

Spiritual Gifts, for example, are distributed at the discretion of the Holy Spirit. They are unique to you, customized to your personality, temperament, etc. Your gift is so designed for excellence that if you stir up the gift within you and seek to perfect it, it will operate on the level of excellence for which it was intended. The problem enters in when the system of human

23

evaluation is placed on the spiritual gifts, ascribing a "pyramid of value;" some gifts more valuable than others, therefore, some more desirable than others; or the different administrations of the same gift having differing levels of esteem. Here stalks the lion of malicious envy, a negative emotional influence that ruins a person and his/her mind causing the envious person to blindly want the object of their envy to suffer in some way. They may not want the person to step in front of a bus, but maybe that the sound system die in the middle of their sermon; or let them get stuck in traffic or have a flat causing them to miss the TV taping.

Listen to the conversation between Rev. Green and the Holy Spirit as human value enters the picture in the case of Rev. Green and Rev. White. Notice how Rev. Green was focused on Rev. White's spiritual gift.

Rev. Green: Rev. White has a powerful teaching ministry. Her gift of teaching comes through in her sermons. I wish I had the gift of teaching that Rev. White has. I want to be able to write and deliver teaching sermons.

Holy Spirit: Teaching is not the gift I've given you. I've given you the gift of healing. How will you use it?

Rev. Green: Yeah, but I want that gift of teaching. I can do it just as good, if not better than Rev. White.

Holy Spirit: No you can't do it better. That's not the gift I've given you. I've given you the gift of healing.

Rev. Green: Yeah, but I want that gift of teaching. I like it better. I know I can do it. Hmmm. In fact, I don't really need Rev. White on staff anymore. I can handle the teaching ministry myself.

When the Holy Spirit called Rev. Green's attention to the gift of healing, Rev. Green never acknowledged his own gift.

He recognized that Rev. White was doing a great job so the envy wasn't negative or personally against Rev. White at first. Rev. Green saw something he admired in another preacher. Nothing wrong with that – but he didn't stop there. Sin pushed him into a downward spiral heading straight toward the danger zone. Admiration took a back seat to covetousness, a desire to have what Rev. White had. Finally, instead of recognizing the gift of healing in himself and devising a plan to develop his gift, his plan was to dismiss Rev. White and operate in the gift he wanted instead of the gift he was divinely given. Envy can become negative and personal causing you to enter the danger zone.

You may honestly and without malice admire something another preacher has, a charismatic delivery, abilities, a bigger church, a more supportive congregation. Admiration is honorable. Just be cautious. Envy can turn into a sneaky foe. Admiration can fall prey to envy with covetousness wherein you no longer admire but you desire. Now you have a problem. If you don't bring that feeling under subjection to the Holy Spirit you'll find yourself consumed with the desire and taking steps to get what they have.

Envy doesn't always start out as admiration and desire to emulate. Sometimes envy starts out bad. You've heard of preachers, or perhaps even known one or two who envied the advantages, possessions, notoriety of a colleague, things they desired but lacked. They undermined the ministry of a colleague in order to take it. In the secular world, it's called "back stabbing." In the realm of the ecclesia, there is no holy word for it, it's simply "back stabbing."

When Others Envy You

You may find yourself the focus of another preacher's envy, benign or malicious. Always keep your humility meter fine-tuned through prayerful relationship with God. There are three things you must do when you become aware of envy by a colleague: (1) Keep your head on straight; (2) Commit the matter to prayer; and (3) Keep a safe distance. Take the high road and assume there is no malice intended but you can see how quickly one can go from the safety zone to the danger zone when envy degrades from admiration to covetousness. You have a responsibility to use wisdom to protect yourself. Remember the roaring lion is seeking to devour. Your admirer might suddenly get hungry. You've seen others in the danger zone and you don't want to fall victim to that. To be the object of someone's admiration is affirming and feels nice. Everyone needs affirmation from time to time. Just prayerfully remember that the affirmation is for that which God alone has placed in you. It's the God in you that they see.

JEALOUSY

Jealousy is having the fear that someone is going to take what you have. Jealousy is having the fear and suspicion of losing one's position or situation to someone else. Jealousy has to do with holding on to what you have because you fear that someone else is going to take it away. The operative word is fear. While fear is a vital response to physical and emotional danger, if you didn't feel it, you couldn't protect yourself from legitimate threats, however, fear of loss as defined by jealousy is entirely different. There may or may not be a basis in reality concerning the threat of the loss, but there is certainly a feeling of resentment and generally describes a sort of emotional rivalry between people. When it comes to jealousy, there is no safety zone. When jealousy appears, it takes you in only one direction. Down. Think about it. If you fear that someone can take something,

> Jealousy is the fear that someone is going to take what you have

that describes the feeling of inadequacy. They have the power to take. Jealousy begins to talk to you saying, "You have to fight to keep what you have." Both envy and jealousy breed feelings of inadequacy. When you feel inadequate anger sets in and everyone around you becomes actors in your play.

When You're Jealous of Someone

Real or imagined, you perceive someone has the power to take something away from you. You become distracted from your work and focused on the fight. That person becomes your rival. Even if it's only in your mind, your perception is your reality and you act accordingly. Follow this short hypothetical scenario:

There's a young, very gifted preacher on your staff. People are excited about him, saying what a good preacher he is, great personality, on and on. They're even saying that you should allow him to preach more often on Sundays, maybe even give him one Sunday a month. You may not recognize it at first but you feel a little something stirring up on the inside. Jealousy is beginning to take root as it did with Saul toward David.

Your imagination gets the better of you and you begin to imagine the preacher is trying to undermine you, steal the affections of your people until he steals "your" church. Little by little you find yourself identifying faults in the young associate. You're becoming less friendly toward him, less encouraging and more critical of him. When others speak of him you find fault. You begin to cut back on his responsibilities for no real reason other than the fact that you have the power to do it, until finally the young preacher leaves.

The kingdom reality is this. What God has for you is for you. No one can take anything away from you that God has

27

given to you. You can give it away by being ungrateful, mediocre, or by succumbing to jealousy, but no one can take it. That doesn't mean they won't try; it just means they won't succeed. Suppose they can preach better, teach better, possess better skills in other areas of leadership. So what! You have what it takes for your divine assignment. If more were required, you would have been given more. "Do you." Be your best "you."

When Someone is Jealous of You

When you're the object of someone's jealousy, you're in a very dangerous position. You're in the crosshair of the "fiery darts of the wicked." Don't try to rationalize it or look for logic. There is none. If their jealousy of you goes unchecked, it will only degrade. It isn't the same as being the object of an admirer's envy (Envy in the Safe Zone). Be very clear about this. Jealousy is a murderer. Jealousy would claim self-defense but that plea would never stand the scrutiny of the Holy Spirit. Jealousy commits premeditated murder; spiritual murder in the 1st degree. The one guilty of murder by jealousy is guilty of the included lesser charges: anger, malicious envy, hatred, meanness, plotting, as well. It's most formidable weapon is the tongue; with the tongue, it can take you out. Jealousy will try to hurt you, demean you, embarrass you, discourage you, exclude you, eliminate you, destroy your reputation, undermine your work. Jealousy will do anything that will take you out of its equation.

Murder by Jealousy

[Spiritual]

1st Degree Murder

A person's jealousy toward you is not your fault. The problem lies within that person. You, however, as the object of another's jealousy, do have a threefold responsibility. (1) Compassion wants you to understand a jealous person isn't a bad person, but they are an insecure person. The seed of their insecurities were planted long before you ever came on the scene. Don't take it too personally. You're just a convenient target. There were others before you and there will be others after you. They would be jealous of almost anyone. Think of how it must feel to have an emotion that rises up within and gets out of hand. Jealousy doesn't travel alone; it's companions are envy, anger, spite, hatred, just to name a few. For a colleague to be jealous of another, it can't be a good feeling. No one enjoys being out of control. Being ruled by any emotion can't be a pleasant experience. In the midnight hour, in those dark quiet moments when no one else is around, even if but for a moment, the jealous person is not proud but rather ashamed of their feelings. That's not to say it's okay. It's just reminder that compassion has a voice in this matter.

Secondly, your responsibility is to protect yourself and your purpose. Within the context of this concern you can't make someone not be jealous but you can guard yourself if or when you find that you're the object of their jealousy. Of course, you cover the matter in prayer. It's bigger than you are. Jealousy has far too many warrior companions for you to deal with alone. Be smart and keep a safe distance from a jealous person. You can't fix jealousy. You can't love jealousy away, or love someone out of their jealousy. Step back! This demon is for the Holy Ghost alone.

Thirdly, keep watch on your "humility meter." Make sure you aren't doing anything to kindle the flame of jealousy in another person. Watch your mouth to make sure you aren't bragging in any way. Make sure your verbal praise and thanksgiving isn't a veneer for bragging. Humility says, "Whatever good is in me, I'm grateful to God for it and for the privilege of using it to God's glory." Paul says it's God who has begun the good work in you and it's God who performs it through you. Keep your head on straight.

Finally, this closing thought about jealousy. Jealousy is, above all things, an extreme lack of faith in God. It speaks loudly in one's spirit saying:

- God has given you less than someone else
- Someone else is better
- What God has given is insufficient
- God will allow someone to take what you have.

Jealousy doesn't see the big picture; the purpose God for bringing people into each other's lives. Jealousy is insecure and selfish, thinking only of itself and what it stands to lose.

NOTES

1. Are you jealous of someone today? If so, why? Be honest.

_____

_____

_____

_____

2. What does a jealous spirit say about one's perception of God?

_____

_____

_____

_____

3. Note three scriptures that address the matter of jealousy.

_____

_____

_____

_____

ENVY & JEALOUSY	
ENVY 2 Entities At least 2 people	**JEALOUSY** 3 Entities 2+ people & 1 object of desire
You Want Something Someone Else Has	**Afraid Someone Is Going To Take What You Have**
Doesn't always carry a negative connotation	Always implies a feeling of resentment toward another.
Can be used to show a desire to equal another in achievement or excellence as in emulation. Desire to emulate doesn't have negative connotations.	Always negative
A reaction to lacking something	A reaction to the threat of losing something (church; notoriety)
The emotion when you want a position or notoriety that someone else has	The emotion when you fear you may be replaced in the affection of the people you love
To bear a grudge toward someone due to coveting what that person has or enjoys	Apprehensive or vengeful out of fear of being replaced by someone else.
In a milder sense: the longing for something someone else has without any ill will intended toward that person	It can also mean watchful, or anxiously suspicious.
When one lacks a desired attribute of another person.	When something we already have is threatened by another.

THE TEN COMMANDMENTS OF EXCELLENCE		
1st	THOU SHALL KEEP THY HEAD ON STRAIGHT	Regularly check for the EGW virus
2nd	THOU SHALL BE THINE AUTHENTIC SELF	Be not guilty of "Identity Theft"
3rd	THOU SHALL LINK TO THE CLOUD	Make prayer your Homepage
4th	THOU SHALL WISELY CHOOSE THY INNER CIRCLE	You are the average of the five people with whom you spend the most time
5th	THOU SHALL FLEE JEALOUSY & ENVY	You can be a victim or an offender
6th	THOU SHALL NOT KILL	Watch your mouth!
7th	THOU SHALL DO THY HOMEWORK THOROUGHLY	Be the standard bearer for excellence
8th	THOU SHALL NOT STEAL	Be a person of integrity. Don't steal. Give credit.
9th	THOU SHALL KNOW THY DEMONS	They know you!
10th	THOU SHALL TRAVEL LIGHT	Check your bags regularly. Unpack regularly. Keep only what you need.

ABOUT THE AUTHOR

$\mathcal{CL}$. LAWRENCE, LEADERSHIP DEVELOPMENT STRATEGIST, a dynamic Christian communicator best known for her eclectic approach to teaching and preaching the Word of God and distinctive gift of discovering contemporary insights in the Biblical stories while maintaining the integrity of the Biblical text. Her passion for excellence has made her a much sought after conference speaker, seminar facilitator. Exciting. Thought provoking. Empowering, are words used to describe her ministry "Boot Camps," and other events. She combines a 12-year tenure in Corporate America with 30+ years of pastoral and church leadership.

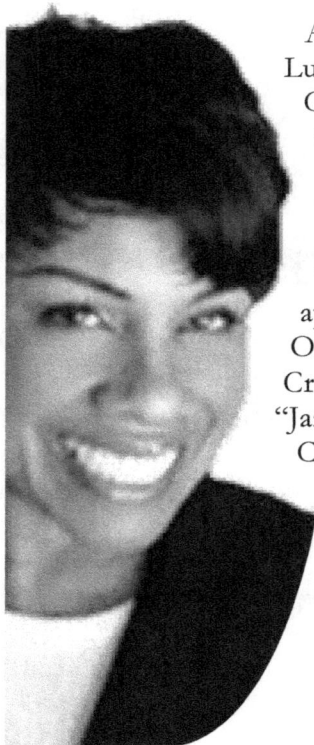

A graduate of Cheyney University, Lutheran Theological Seminary and Tony Campolo School for Social Change, Carol is the founder of Lawrence Seminars, Inc., Host of Empowerment Gatherings (worship/ networking events); and Teacher/Facilitator of "Women at the Well" (a unique approach to Bible Study for Women Only). A.K.A. "ZseZse," she's the Creator, Host and Producer of the podcast "Jazz Divine; Zse-votions, (devotional CDs); and her Blogcast, "Just Thinking."

To book an engagement
Email:
CLL@LawrenceMinistries.com
Visit:
LawrenceMinisties.com

34

Visit C.L. Lawrence on:
Amazon.com/Author/CLLawrence
&
Kindle.com

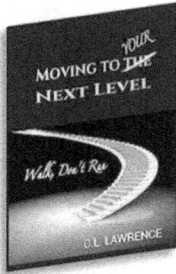

MOVING TO YOUR NEXT LEVEL
WALK, DON'T RUN

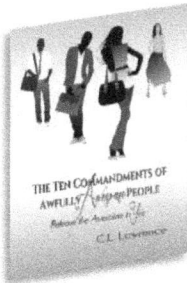

THE TEN COMMANDMENTS
OF AWFULLY AWESOME PEOPLE
RELEASE THE AWESOME IN YOU!

DIAMONDS IN THE ROUGH
NAVIGATING THROUGH
NO MAN'S LAND
FOR ASSOCIATE MINISTERS